Twenty to **Knit**

Pocket Pets

Sachiyo Ishii

Search Press

Dedication

*I would like to dedicate this book to my
dear cousin, Hiroko Yamada, with whom
I share lots of childhood memories.*

First published in 2019

Search Press Limited
Wellwood, North Farm Road,
Tunbridge Wells, Kent TN2 3DR

Text copyright © Sachiyo Ishii 2019

Photographs by Fiona Murray

Photographs and design copyright
© Search Press Ltd. 2019

ISBN: 978-1-78221-695-7

Publisher's Note

The Publishers and author can accept no
responsibility for any consequences arising from
the information, advice or instructions given in
this publication.

Readers are permitted to reproduce any
of the items in this book for their personal use,
or for the purposes of selling for charity, free of
charge and without the prior permission of the
Publishers. Any use of the items for commercial
purposes is not permitted without the prior
permission of the Publishers.

Suppliers

If you have difficulty in obtaining any of
the materials and equipment mentioned
in this book, then please visit the Search Press
website for details of suppliers:
www.searchpress.com

Contents

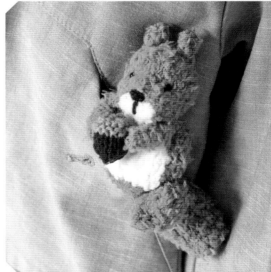

Introduction

We all like small fluffy creatures. I remember when my children were young, we used to enjoy going to the farmyard on open days to have cuddles with baby animals. Having never kept pets at home, my boys felt nervous, even a little scared of holding animals. However, they didn't seem to mind the chicks. I remember them cupping their hands to hold a little bird and gently stroking its feathers.

Although it is not made from natural fibres, I've always had a weak spot for fleecy yarn. It feels so soft and fluffy. Maybe it reminds me of the chicks at the farmyard. Creating little animals with fleecy yarn came very naturally to me. I just could not resist.

My first project was a tiny, chubby mouse with the body and head knitted together. It was simple but I found the result completely adorable. Creating something cute using such a small quantity of yarn is utterly delightful. The knitting was very easy and quick, so I had to make more.

This book is a collection of little pets that you can carry in your pocket. They can travel with you and entertain you whether you are travelling by a car, train or aeroplane. They are perfect for small hands.

You may find that fleecy yarn is not the easiest to knit with at the beginning. You cannot see stitches clearly and it is hard to recover a dropped stitch, but do not worry. Count your stitches from time to time and if you notice you have increased or decreased by accident, simply fix it on the next row. Making up is one of the challenges for beginners, but the seams are not visible with this yarn and the toys will have a lovely, neat finish. Intrigued?

Happy knitting!

Knitting know-how

Yarn

The animals are knitted with fleecy yarn in DK (8-ply/light worsted) weight. You don't need much yarn to create each toy. Some of them require less than 5m (5.5yd).

Most fleecy yarn comes in two different weights; DK (8-ply/light worsted) and chunky (bulky). Even though two types of yarn may be categorized as the same weight, their thickness and yardage may differ depending on the brand. You may prefer one brand to another, so try several to find your favourite. If you want to make larger animals, you can use chunky (bulky) weight yarn and larger needles, without having to change the patterns. Most of the animals are knitted using yarn with a yardage of 25g per 83–85m (91–93yd).

Tiny amounts of ordinary DK (8-ply/light worsted) yarn and 4-ply (fingering) yarn are used for the smaller body parts, such as ears and feet, and also embroidering features, such as noses and mouths. If you need to buy yarn, tapestry yarn is a good choice because it comes in small amounts and a huge variety of colours.

Stuffing

I have used polyester toy stuffing, which is readily available from most craft shops and online craft stores.

Beads

4–6mm (⅛–¼in) beads are used as eyes for a few of the projects. I prefer to use beads with threading holes and attach them after the head is stuffed; however, if you are making an animal for a child, you may prefer to use safety eyes. If you are using this type, attach them before stuffing the head. Alternatively, you can embroider French knots with DK (8-ply/light worsted) yarn.

Knitting needles

Throughout the book I used 3.5mm (UK 9 or 10, US 4) needles for the fleecy DK (8-ply/light worsted) yarn, and 3mm (UK 11, US 2 or 3) needles for regular DK (8-ply/light worsted) yarn. I always use bamboo needles as they are less slippery than metal ones and keep your stitches neat and even. Your knitting tension (gauge) needs to be fairly tight, so that when toys are sewn up, the stuffing is not visible through the stitches. If you struggle with knitting fleecy yarn on these needle sizes, experiment with larger needles. Some knitters knit more tightly than others and the tension (gauge) also differs depending on the yarn you use. I have given a general tension (gauge) guide below, but tensions are not specified for any of the projects, as the size of the finished items doesn't really matter.

Sewing your work together

I recommend that you use a chenille or tapestry needle with a sharp point, as it is easier to work through your tightly knitted toys than using a blunt-ended needle. You can also use the same needle for embroidering features on the toys. Your toys will be sewn up using the same yarn that you knitted them with, so it is a good idea to make a habit of leaving fairly long yarn ends when you cast on and cast off. Join the seams using mattress stitch with right sides facing outwards.

Stuffing the toys

These knitted pieces can be quite stretchy. Stuff them relatively lightly to keep the finished toys nice and soft.

Shaping

It is not for all projects, but I find some of the faces look more attractive with an indentation for the eyes. With the fleecy yarn used for the head, work a gathering thread over the eyeline and pull gently to shape it.

Tension (gauge)

I worked to a tension of 22 stitches x 26 rows = 10cm (4in) measured over stocking stitch (US stockinette stitch); however, it is not essential to stick to this.

Other tools

Wooden chopstick

A simple but incredibly effective tool, a chopstick is by far the best instrument for pushing stuffing into your toys. If you don't have one, you could use a large knitting needle or a pencil.

Scissors

A pair of sharp scissors is essential for trimming yarn ends when sewing up your projects.

Needle threader

This is not essential but I find it useful to help thread yarn on to my needle when I am sewing up projects.

Row counter

This can be useful to keep count of your rows when you are working with fleecy yarn, as it's sometimes difficult to see them.

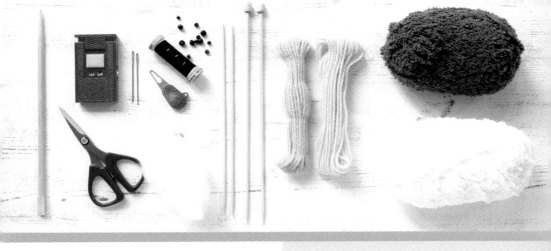

Techniques

I-cord

I-cords are used for some of the body parts. Using DPN, cast on the required number of stitches. Do not turn. Slide the stitches to the opposite end of the needle, then knit the stitches again, taking the yarn firmly across the back of the work. Repeat to the desired length. Break yarn and thread through the stitches or cast off, as instructed in the pattern.

Embroidery

French knots

These are used for many of the figures' and animals' eyes. Thread your needle with yarn and bring it up from the back where you want to make a knot. Holding the needle firmly, wrap the yarn around it twice. Push the needle through to the back of the project, leaving the French knot on the surface.

Abbreviations

The abbreviations listed below are the most frequently used terms in the book. Any special abbreviations in a pattern are explained on the relevant page.

beg	beginning
cm	centimetres
DK	double knitting
DPN	double-pointed needle(s)
g	grams
g st	garter stitch
inc	increase
in(s)	inch(es)
k	knit
kfb	knit into the front and back of the stitch, making one more stitch
k2tog	knit 2 stitches together
k3tog	knit 3 stitches together
m	metres
mm	millimetres
oz	ounces
p	purl
pfb	purl into the front and back of the stitch, making one more stitch
p2tog	purl 2 stitches together
rep	repeat
RS	right side(s)
skpo	slip 1, knit 1, pass the slipped stitch over
sl1	slip one stitch from the left-hand needle to the right-hand needle without working it
st(s)	stitch(es)
st st	stocking stitch (US stockinette stitch)
tog	together
WS	wrong sides(s)
yb	yarn back
yf	yarn forward
yd	yard(s)

Polar Bear

Materials:

10g (⅖oz) of fleecy DK (8-ply/light worsted) yarn in white (A)

Small amount of DK (8-ply/light worsted) yarn in dark brown (B)

Small amounts of felted tweed DK (8-ply/light worsted) yarn in red or blue (C)

Toy stuffing

Tools:

3.5mm (UK 9 or 10, US 4) needles and 3mm (UK 11, US 2 or 3) needles

Stitch holder

Size:

11cm (4¼in) tall

Instructions:

Body
First leg

Using yarn A and 3.5mm (UK 9 or 10, US 4) needles, cast on 7 sts.

Row 1 (WS): p to end.

Row 2: (kfb) to end (14 sts).

Rows 3–7: beg with a p row, work 5 rows in st st.

Break off yarn and place sts on a stitch holder.

Second leg

Work the second leg in the same way, but do not break off the yarn.

With RS facing, work across both legs to join.

Row 8: k14 (from the second leg), cast on 3 sts, k14 (from the first leg) (31 sts).

Row 9: cast on 3 sts. p to end (34 sts).

Rows 10–27: beg with a k row, work 18 rows in st st.

Row 28: cast off 8 sts, k1, (k2, k2tog) four times, cast off remaining 8 sts (14 sts).

Row 29: rejoin yarn A, cast on 8 sts, p to end (22 sts).

Row 30: cast on 8 sts, k to end (30 sts).

Rows 31–34: beg with a p row, work 4 rows in st st.

Row 35: p16, turn.

Row 36: sl1, k1, turn.
Row 37: sl1, p2, turn.
Row 38: sl1, k3, turn.
Row 39: sl1, p4, turn.
Row 40: sl1, k5, turn.
Row 41: sl1, p6, turn.
Row 42: sl1, k7, turn.
Row 43: sl1, p8, turn.
Row 44: sl1, k9, turn.
Row 45: sl1, p10, turn.
Row 46: sl1, k11, turn.
Row 47: sl1, p12, turn.
Row 48: sl1, k13, turn.
Row 49: sl1, p14, turn.
Row 50: sl1, k15, turn.
Row 51: sl1, p16, turn.
Row 52: sl1, k17, turn.
Row 53: p to end (30 sts).

Rows 54–60: beg with a k row, work 7 rows in st st.

Cast off.

Ears: make two

Using yarn A and 3.5mm (UK 9 or 10, US 4) needles, cast on 10 sts and purl 1 row.

Break yarn, draw through sts, pull tightly and fasten off.

Sew the ends together to make a semi-circle.

Nose

Using yarn B and 3mm (UK 11, US 2 or 3) needles, cast on 16 sts.

Break yarn, draw through sts, pull tightly and fasten off.

Sew the ends together to make a bobble.

Scarf

Using yarn C and 3mm (UK 11, US 2 or 3) needles, cast on 4 sts and work in g st until scarf measures 24cm (9½in).

Cast off.

To make up

Using the cast-on yarn end, work a gathering thread along the cast-on edge of each leg and draw up tightly. Sew each leg seam to the crotch.

Sew up the back seam to the cast-off edge created at row 28. Fold each arm horizontally and sew each arm from the tip. Work a gathering thread along the tip of each arm and draw up tightly to close.

Stuff the arms, legs and body. Sew the cast-off edge of the body to the cast-off edge created at row 28, leaving a gap for stuffing the head. Stuff the head, pushing the stuffing up firmly. Close the gap.

Attach the ears and nose. Using yarn B, embroider French knots for the eyes and embroider a mouth with a straight stitch. Add small tassels to both ends of the scarf and tie the scarf around the neck.

Chicks

Materials:

To make one:

Small amount of fleecy DK (8-ply/light worsted) yarn in yellow (A)

Small amounts of DK (8-ply/light worsted) yarn in dark yellow (B), light brown (C) and dark brown (D)

Toy stuffing

Needles:

3.5mm (UK 9 or 10, US 4) needles, 3mm (UK 11, US 2 or 3) needles and 3mm (UK 11, US 2 or 3) DPN

Size:

5cm (2in) tall

Instructions:

Body

Using yarn A and 3.5mm (UK 9 or 10, US 4) needles, cast on 10 sts.

Row 1 (WS): p to end.

Row 2: (kfb) to end (20 sts).

Rows 3–11: beg with a p row, work 9 rows in st st.

Row 12: k2tog, (k1, k2tog) to end (13 sts).

Rows 13–16: beg with a p row, work 4 rows in st st.

Break yarn, draw through sts, pull tightly and fasten off.

Beak

Using yarn B and 3mm (UK 11, US 2 or 3) needles, cast on 5 sts.

Row 1 (WS): p2tog, p1, p2tog (3 sts).

Row 2: sl1, k2tog, pass the first st over the second st and fasten off.

Feet: make two

Using yarn B and 3mm (UK 11, US 2 or 3) needles, cast on 5 sts.

Row 1: k to end.

Row 2: skpo, k1, k2tog (3 sts).

Row 3: sl1, k2tog, pass the first st over the second st and fasten off.

Legs: make two

Using yarn C and 3mm (UK 11, US 2 or 3) DPN, cast on 3 sts and work an i-cord for 5 rows.

Break yarn, draw through sts, pull tightly and fasten off.

To make up

Using the fastened-off yarn end, sew the body seam and stuff. Using the cast-on yarn end, work a gathering thread along the cast-on edge and draw up tightly to close the body.

Attach the cast-on edge of the beak to the body. Attach the feet to the legs and then attach the legs to the body. Using yarn D, embroider French knots for the eyes.

Koala Bear

Materials:

5g (⅕oz) of fleecy DK (8-ply/light worsted) yarn in grey (A) and a small amount in white (B)

Small amount of 4-ply (fingering) yarn in dark brown (C)

Two 4mm (⅛in) black beads

Black cotton thread

Toy stuffing

Needles:

3.5mm (UK 9 or 10, US 4) needles

Size:

8cm (3⅛in) tall

Instructions:

Body

Using yarn A, cast on 20 sts.

Rows 1–8: beg with a k (RS) row, work 8 rows in st st.

Row 9: cast off 4 sts, k to end (16 sts).

Row 10: cast off 4 sts, p to end (12 sts).

Row 11: cast on 2 sts, k to end (14 sts).

Row 12: cast on 2 sts, p to end (16 sts).

Rows 13 and 14: beg with a k row, work 2 rows in st st.

Row 15: cast off 2 sts, k to end (14 sts).

Row 16: cast off 2 sts, p to end (12 sts).

Row 17: cast on 4 sts, k to end (16 sts).

Row 18: cast on 4 sts, p to end (20 sts).

Rows 19–23: beg with a k row, work 5 rows in st st. Cast off.

Head

Using yarn A, cast on 10 sts.

Row 1 (WS): p to end.

Row 2: (kfb) to end (20 sts).

Rows 3–7: beg with a p row, work 5 rows in st st.

Row 8 (eyeline): k5, (k2tog) five times, k5 (15 sts).

Rows 9–11: beg with a p row, work 3 rows in st st.

Row 12: (k1, k2tog) to end (10 sts).

Row 13: p to end.

Row 14: (k1, k2tog), k1 (7 sts).

Break yarn, draw through sts, pull tightly and fasten off.

Ears: make two

Using yarn A, cast on 12 sts.

Row 1 (WS): p7 (A), join in yarn B, p5 (B).

Row 2: keeping colours correct, k to end.

Row 3: p2 (A), p2tog (A), p1 (A), p2tog (A), p2 (B), p2tog (B), p1 (B) (9 sts).

Break off yarn B and continue using yarn A only.

Row 4: (k2tog, k1) to end (6 sts).

Break yarn, draw through sts, pull tightly and fasten off.

To make up

Fold each leg horizontally and sew each leg from the tip. Work a gathering thread along the tip of each leg and pull tightly to close. Repeat for the arms. Stuff the arms and legs. Sew up the tummy seam leaving a gap for stuffing. Stuff and close the body.

Using the fastened-off yarn end, sew up the head seam to half way. Using the cast-on yarn end, work a gathering thread along the cast-on edge and draw up tightly. Stuff the head and close the seam.

Using yarn A, work a gathering thread over the eyeline and pull gently to shape. Sew each ear seam and attach the cast-on edge of the ears to the head. Attach the beads for the eyes. Using yarn C, embroider a nose with straight stitches. Attach the head to the body.

Fox

Materials:

5g (⅛oz) of fleecy DK (8-ply/light worsted) yarn in orange (A) and small amounts in white (B) and black (C)

Small amount of DK (8-ply/light worsted) yarn in dark brown (D)

Toy stuffing

Needles:

3.5mm (UK 9 or 10, US 4) needles

Size:

15cm (6in) long including tail

Instructions:

Body

Using yarn A, cast on 10 sts.

Row 1 (WS): p to end.

Row 2: (kfb) to end (20 sts).

Rows 3–13: beg with a p row, work 11 rows in st st.

Row 14: (k2, k2tog) to end (15 sts).

Rows 15–21: beg with a p row, work 7 rows in st st.

Row 22: (k1, k2tog) to end (10 sts).

Row 23: p to end.

Break yarn, draw through sts, pull tightly and fasten off.

Head

Using yarn A, cast on 9 sts.

Row 1 (WS): p to end.

Row 2: (kfb) to end (18 sts).

Rows 3–5: beg with a p row, work 3 rows in st st.

Row 6: join in yarn B, k5 (B), k8 (A), join in another strand of yarn B, k5 (B).

Rows 7–9: keeping colours correct and beg with a p row, work 3 rows in st st.

Row 10 (eyeline): keeping colours correct, k5, (k2tog) four times, k5 (14 sts).

Row 11: keeping colours correct, p to end.

Row 12: keeping colours correct, k1, (k2tog) twice, k4, (k2tog) twice, k1 (10 sts).

Rows 13–14: keeping colours correct and beg with a p row, work 2 rows in st st.

Row 15: keeping colours correct, p1, (p2tog) four times, p1 (6 sts).

Break yarns and using yarn B, draw through sts, pull tightly and fasten off.

Tail

Using yarn A, cast on 12 sts.

Row 1 (RS): join in yarn B, k2 (B), k8 (A), join in another strand of yarn B, k2 (B).

Rows 2–8: keeping colours correct and beg with a p row, work 7 rows in st st.

Row 9: k2 (B), k2tog (A), k4 (A), k2tog (A), k2 (B) (10 sts).

Row 10: keeping colours correct, p to end.

Row 11: keeping colours correct, k4, k2tog, k4 (9 sts).

Rows 12–13: keeping colours correct, beg with a p row, work 2 rows in st st.

Row 14: keeping colours correct, p2tog, p5, p2tog (7 sts).

Break off yarn B and continue using yarn A only.

Row 15: k1, (k2tog) to end (4 sts).

Break yarn, draw through sts, pull tightly and fasten off.

Ears: make two

Using yarn A, cast on 5 sts.

Row 1: skpo, k1, k2tog (3 sts).

Row 2: k to end.

Row 3: sl1, k2tog, pass the first st over the second st and fasten off.

Front legs: make two

Using yarn C, cast on 7 sts.

Rows 1–3: beg with a p (WS) row, work 3 rows in st st.

Break off yarn C.

Rows 4–8: change to yarn A and beg with a k row, work 5 rows in st st.

Cast off.

Hind legs: make two

Using yarn C, cast on 8 sts and work as for the front legs.

To make up

Using the fastened-off yarn end, sew up the body seam to half way. Using the cast-on yarn end, work a gathering thread along the cast-on edge and draw up tightly. Sew up the body seam a little further, stuff and close the body.

Using matching yarn, make up the head in the same way as the body. Using yarn A, work a gathering thread over the eyeline and pull gently to shape. Using yarn D, embroider French knots for the eyes and embroider a nose with straight stitches. Attach the cast-on edge of the ears to the head. Attach the head to the body.

Using the cast-on yarn end, work a gathering thread along the cast-on edge of each leg and draw up tightly. Using matching yarn, sew the leg seams and stuff. Attach the cast-off edges of the legs to the body. Beginning at the fastened-off end, sew the tail seam. With the seam underneath the tail, attach the cast-on edge to the body without stuffing.

Teddy Bear

Materials:

10g (⅖oz) of fleecy DK (8-ply/light worsted) yarn in light brown (A)

Small amount of DK (8-ply/light worsted) yarn in dark brown (B)

Two 4mm (⅛in) black beads

Black cotton thread

Toy stuffing

1 x 26cm (½in x 10¼in) length of red ribbon

Needles:

3.5mm (UK 9 or 10, US 4) needles

Size:

10cm (4in) tall

Instructions:

Body

Using yarn A, cast on 20 sts.

Rows 1–10: beg with a k (RS) row, work 10 rows in st st.

Row 11: cast off 4 sts, k to end (16 sts).

Row 12: cast off 4 sts, p to end (12 sts).

Row 13: cast on 2 sts, k to end (14 sts).

Row 14: cast on 2 sts, p to end (16 sts).

Rows 15 and 16: beg with a k row, work 2 rows in st st.

Row 17: cast off 2 sts, k to end (14 sts).

Row 18: cast off 2 sts, p to end (12 sts).

Row 19: cast on 4 sts, k to end (16 sts).

Row 20: cast on 4 sts, p to end (20 sts).

Rows 21–28: beg with a k row, work 8 rows in st st.

Row 29: cast off 4 sts, k to end (16 sts).

Cast off.

Head

Using yarn A, cast on 7 sts.

Row 1 (WS): p to end.

Row 2: (kfb) to end (14 sts).

Row 3: p to end.

Row 4: (k1, kfb) to end (21 sts).

Rows 5–11: beg with a p row, work 7 rows in st st.

Row 12 (eyeline): k5, (k2tog) five times, k6 (16 sts).

Row 13: p to end.

Row 14: k4, (k2tog) four times, k4 (12 sts).

Row 15: p to end.

Row 16: (k2tog) to end (6 sts).

Break yarn, draw through sts, pull tightly and fasten off.

Ears: make two

Using yarn A, cast on 8 sts.

Row 1: purl.

Break yarn, draw through sts, pull tightly and fasten off.

Sew the ends together to make a semi-circle.

To make up

Fold each leg horizontally and sew each leg from the tip. Work a gathering thread along the tip of each leg and draw up tightly to close. Repeat for the arms. Stuff the arms and legs. Sew up the tummy seam leaving a gap for stuffing. Stuff and close the body.

Using the fastened-off yarn end, sew up the head seam to half way. Using the cast-on yarn end, work a gathering thread along the cast-on edge and draw up tightly. Stuff the head and close the seam. Using yarn A, work a gathering thread over the eyeline and pull gently to shape. Attach the ears. Attach the beads for the eyes. Using yarn B, embroider a nose with straight stitches. Attach the head to the body. Tie the ribbon around the neck.

Guinea Pig

Materials:

7g (¼oz) of fleecy DK (8-ply/light worsted) yarn in light brown (A) and a small amount in white (B)

Small amount of 4-ply (fingering) yarn in brown (C)

Two 4mm (⅛in) black beads

Black cotton thread

Toy stuffing

Needles:

3.5mm (UK 9 or 10, US 4) needles

Size:

9.5cm (3¾in) long

Instructions:

Body

Using yarn A, cast on 12 sts.

Row 1 (WS): p to end.

Row 2: (kfb) to end (24 sts).

Rows 3–15: beg with a p row, work 13 rows in st st.

Row 16: cast off 2 sts, k to end (22 sts).

Row 17: cast off 2 sts, p to end (20 sts).

Row 18: cast on 2 sts, knit these 2 sts, k9, (kfb) twice, k9 (24 sts).

Row 19: cast on 2 sts, p to end (26 sts).

Row 20: k12, (kfb) twice, k to end (28 sts).

Row 21: p to end.

Row 22: cast off 2 sts, k to end (26 sts).

Row 23: cast off 2 sts, p to end (24 sts).

Row 24: join in yarn B, k5 (B), k14 (A), join in another strand of yarn B, k5 (B).

Row 25: p6 (B), p12 (A), p6 (B).

Row 26: cast off 4 sts (B), k2 (B), k4 (A), k2 (B), k4 (A), k7 (B) (20 sts).

Row 27: cast off 4 sts (B), p2 (B), p3 (A), p4 (B), p3 (A), p3 (B) (16 sts).

Row 28: k3 (B), k2 (A), k6 (B), k2 (A), k3 (B).

Break off yarn A and continue using yarn B only.

Row 29: p to end.

Row 30: (k2, k2tog) to end (12 sts). Break yarn, draw through sts, pull tightly and fasten off.

Ears: make two

Using yarn A, cast on 6 sts.

Row 1 (WS): p to end.

Row 2: k2, k2tog, k2 (5 sts).

Break yarn, draw through sts, pull tightly and fasten off.

To make up

Using the fastened-off yarn end, sew the seam from the nose to the chest. Using the cast-on yarn end, work a gathering thread along the cast-on edge and draw up tightly. Sew up the tummy seam leaving a gap for stuffing.

Fold each front leg horizontally and sew each front leg from the tip. Work a gathering thread along the tip of each front leg and draw up tightly to close. Stuff and close the body.

Attach the cast-on edge of the ears to the head. Attach the beads for the eyes. Using yarn C, embroider a nose and a mouth with straight stitches.

Mouse

Materials:

3g (1/10oz) of fleecy DK (8-ply/light worsted) yarn in cream or light brown (A)

Small amount of DK (8-ply/light worsted) yarn in peach (B)

Two 4mm (1/8in) black beads

Black cotton thread

Toy stuffing

Needles:

3.5mm (UK 9 or 10, US 4) needles, 3mm (UK 11, US 2 or 3) needles and 3mm (UK 11, US 2 or 3) DPN

Size:

6cm (2¼in) long excluding tail

Instructions:

Body

Using yarn A and 3.5mm (UK 9 or 10, US 4) needles, cast on 9 sts.

Row 1 (WS): p to end.

Row 2: (kfb) to end (18 sts).

Row 3: p to end.

Row 4: (k1, kfb) to end (27 sts).

Rows 5–14: beg with a p row, work 10 rows in st st.

Row 15: (p1, p2tog) to end (18 sts).

Rows 16 and 17: beg with a k row, work 2 rows in st st.

Row 18: (k1, k2tog) to end (12 sts).

Rows 19 and 20: beg with a p row, work 2 rows in st st.

Row 21: (p1, p2tog) to end (8 sts).

Break yarn, draw through sts, pull tightly and fasten off.

Ears: make two

Using yarn B and 3mm (UK 11, US 2 or 3) needles, cast on 8 sts and purl 1 row.

Break yarn, draw through sts, pull tightly and fasten off.

Sew the ends together to make a semi-circle.

Tail

Using yarn B and 3mm (UK 11, US 2 or 3) DPN, cast on 3 sts and work an i-cord for 15 rows.

Break yarn, draw through sts, pull tightly and fasten off.

Feet: make four

Using yarn B and 3mm (UK 11, US 2 or 3) DPN, cast on 3 sts and work an i-cord for 2 rows.

Break yarn, draw through sts, pull tightly and fasten off.

To make up

Using the fastened-off yarn end, sew up the body seam to half way. Using the cast-on yarn end, work a gathering thread along the cast-on edge and draw up tightly. Sew up the body seam a little further, stuff and close the body.

Attach the ears, the tail and the feet. Attach the beads for the eyes. Using two strands taken from yarn B, embroider a nose and a mouth with straight stitches.

Baby Penguin

Materials:

5g (⅕oz) of fleecy DK (8-ply/light worsted) yarn in grey (A) and small amounts in black (B) and white (C)

Small amount of DK (8-ply/light worsted) yarn in black (D)

Two 4mm (⅛in) black beads and black cotton thread

Toy stuffing

Needles:

3.5mm (UK 9 or 10, US 4) needles and 3mm (UK 11, US 2 or 3) needles

Size:

8.5cm (3¼in) tall

Instructions:

Body

Using yarn A and 3.5mm (UK 9 or 10, US 4) needles, cast on 10 sts.

Row 1 (WS): p to end.

Row 2: (kfb) to end (20 sts).

Rows 3–19: beg with a p row, work 17 rows in st st.

Row 20: (k2, k2tog) to end (15 sts).

Break off yarn A.

Row 21: join in yarn B, p5 (B), join in yarn C, p5 (C), join in another strand of yarn B, p5 (B).

Rows 22–24: keeping the colours correct and beg with a k row, work 3 rows in st st.

Row 25: p5 (B), p2 (C), p1 (B), p2 (C), p5 (B).

Row 26: keeping the colours correct, k to end.

Break off yarn C and continue using yarn B only.

Rows 27 and 28: beg with a p row, work 2 rows in st st.

Row 29: (p1, p2tog) to end (10 sts).

Break yarn, draw through sts, pull tightly and fasten off.

Wings: make two

Using yarn A and 3.5mm (UK 9 or 10, US 4) needles, cast on 6 sts.

Rows 1–6: k 6 rows.

Row 7: skpo, k to end (5 sts).

Row 8: skpo, k to end (4 sts).

Rows 9 and 10: k 2 rows.

Row 11: skpo, k2 (3 sts).

Break yarn, draw through sts, pull tightly and fasten off.

Beak

Using yarn D and 3mm (UK 11, US 2 or 3) needles, cast on 4 sts.

Row 1 (WS): (p2tog) twice (2 sts).

Row 2: skpo and fasten off.

Feet: make two

Using yarn D and 3mm (UK 11, US 2 or 3) needles, cast on 4 sts.

Rows 1 and 2: k 2 rows.

Row 3: skpo, k2 (3 sts).

Row 4: skpo, k1 (2 sts).

Row 5: k to end.

Row 6: skpo and fasten off.

To make up

Using the fastened-off yarn end, sew up the body seam to half way. Using the cast-on yarn end, work a gathering thread along the cast-on edge and draw up tightly. Using matching yarn, sew up the body seam a little further, stuff and close the body.

Attach the cast-on edge of the wings to the body. Attach the cast-on edge of the beak to the face. Using the fastened-off yarn end, attach the feet. Attach the beads for the eyes.

Mr & Mrs Hamster

Materials:

5g (⅕oz) of fleecy DK (8-ply/light worsted) yarn in khaki brown and brown mix (A) and 3g (⅒oz) in white (B)

Small amounts of DK (8-ply/light worsted) yarn in dark brown (C) and pink (D)

Small amount of 4-ply (fingering) yarn in brown (E)

Toy stuffing

Needles:

3.5mm (UK 9 or 10, US 4) and 3mm (UK 11, US 2 or 3) needles

Size:

10cm (4in) tall

Instructions:

Mr Hamster

Body

Using yarn A and 3.5mm (UK 9 or 10, US 4) needles, cast on 10 sts.

Row 1 (WS): p to end.

Row 2: (kfb) to end (20 sts).

Rows 3–21: beg with a p row, work 19 rows in st st.

Row 22: k6, (k2tog, k1) three times, k5 (17 sts).

Rows 23–27: beg with a p row, work 5 rows in st st.

Row 28: (k2, k2tog) to last st, k1 (13 sts).

Break yarn, draw through sts, pull tightly and fasten off.

Head

Using yarn A and 3.5mm (UK 9 or 10, US 4) needles, cast on 10 sts.

Row 1 (WS): p to end.

Row 2: (kfb) to end (20 sts).

Rows 3–9: beg with a p row, work 7 rows in st st.

Row 10 (eyeline): k5, (k2tog five times, k5 (15 sts).

Row 11: p to end.

Row 12: (k1, k2tog) to end (10 sts).

Row 13: p to end.

Break yarn, draw through sts, pull tightly and fasten off.

Ears: make two

Using yarn D and 3mm (UK 11, US 2 or 3) needles, cast on 8 sts and purl 1 row.

Break yarn, draw through sts, pull tightly and fasten off.

Sew the ends together to make a semi-circle.

Arms: make two

Using yarn A and 3.5mm (UK 9 or 10, US 4) needles, cast on 6 sts.

Rows 1–3: beg with a p (WS) row, work 3 rows in st st.

Row 4: change to yarn D, (k2tog) three times (3 sts).

Break yarn, draw through sts, pull tightly and fasten off.

Feet: make two

Using yarn D and 3mm (UK 11, US 2 or 3) needles, cast on 5 sts.

Rows 1–3: beg with a p (WS) row, work 3 rows in st st.

Break yarn, draw through sts, pull tightly and fasten off.

Tail

Using yarn A and 3.5mm (UK 9 or 10, US 4) needles, cast on 4 sts.

Rows 1–4: beg with a p (WS) row, work 4 rows in st st.

Break yarn, draw through sts, pull tightly and fasten off.

To make up

Using the fastened-off yarn end, sew up the body seam to half way. Using the cast-on yarn end, work a gathering thread along the cast-on edge and draw up tightly. Sew up the body seam a little further, stuff and close the body. Make up the head in the same way as the body.

Using yarn A, work a gathering thread over the eyeline and pull gently to shape. Using yarn C, embroider French knots for the eyes. Using yarn E, embroider a nose and a mouth with straight stitches. Attach the ears to the head and attach the head to the body.

Beginning at the fastened-off end, sew up each arm seam using matching yarn and attach the cast-on end of the arms to the body without stuffing. Using the fastened-off yarn end, sew up each foot seam and attach the cast-on end of the feet to the body without stuffing. Using the fastened-off yarn end, sew the tail seam and attach the cast-on end of the tail to the body without stuffing.

Mrs Hamster

Body

Using yarn B and 3.5mm (UK 9 or 10, US 4) needles, cast on 10 sts and work as for Mr Hamster to row 22 (17 sts).

Change to yarn A and work the rest as for Mr Hamster.

Head

Work as for Mr Hamster.

Ears: make two

Work as for Mr Hamster.

Arms: make two

Using yarn A and 3.5mm (UK 9 or 10, US 4) needles, cast on 6 sts.

Row 1 (WS): p to end.

Rows 2 and 3: change to yarn B and beg with a k row, work 2 rows in st st.

Row 4: change to yarn D, (k2tog) three times (3 sts).

Break yarn, draw through sts, pull tightly and fasten off.

Feet: make two

Work as for Mr Hamster.

Tail

Work as for Mr Hamster.

To make up

Make up as for Mr Hamster using matching yarn.

Bunny

Materials:

4g (⅛oz) of fleecy DK (8-ply/light worsted) yarn in white (A)
Small amount of DK (8-ply/light worsted) yarn in dark brown (B)
Small amount of 4-ply (fingering) yarn in pink (C)
Toy stuffing

Needles:

3.5mm (UK 9 or 10, US 4) needles

Size:

8.5cm (3¼in) tall

Instructions:

Body

Using yarn A, cast on 26 sts.
Rows 1–8: beg with a k (RS) row, work 8 rows in st st.
Row 9: cast off 5 sts, k to end (21 sts).
Row 10: cast off 5 sts, p to end (16 sts).
Row 11: cast on 3 sts, k to end (19 sts).
Row 12: cast on 3 sts, p to end (22 sts).
Rows 13–16: beg with a k row, work 4 rows in st st.
Row 17: k2, (k2tog, k2) to end (17 sts).
Row 18: p to end.
Row 19: cast off 3 sts, k to end (14 sts).
Row 20: cast off 3 sts, p to end (11 sts).
Row 21: cast on 5 sts, k to end (16 sts).
Row 22: cast on 5 sts, p to end (21 sts).
Rows 23–28: beg with a k row, work 6 rows in st st.
Cast off.

Head

Using yarn A, cast on 6 sts.
Row 1 (WS): p to end.

Row 2: (kfb) to end (12 sts).
Rows 3–9: beg with a p row, work 7 rows in st st.
Row 10 (eyeline): k4, (k2tog) twice, k4 (10 sts).
Rows 11–13: beg with a p row, work 3 rows in st st.
Row 14: (k2tog) to end (5 sts).
Break yarn, draw through sts, pull tightly and fasten off.

Ears: make two

Using yarn A, cast on 6 sts.
Rows 1–7: beg with a p (WS) row, work 7 rows in st st.
Row 8: skpo, k2, k2tog (4 sts).
Row 9: p to end.
Row 10: skpo, k2tog, pass the first st over the second st and fasten off.

Tail

Using yarn A, cast on 10 sts.
Rows 1–4: beg with a p (WS) row, work 4 rows in st st.
Break yarn, draw through sts, pull tightly and fasten off.

To make up

Fold each leg horizontally and sew each leg from the tip. Work a gathering thread along the tip of each leg and draw up tightly to close. Repeat for the arms. Stuff the arms and legs. Sew up the tummy seam leaving a gap for stuffing. Stuff and close the body.

Using the fastened-off yarn end, sew up the head seam to half way. Using the cast-on yarn end, work a gathering thread along the cast-on edge and draw up tightly. Stuff the head and close the seam. Using yarn A, work a gathering thread over the eyeline and pull gently to shape. Using yarn B, embroider French knots for the eyes. Using yarn C, embroider a nose and a mouth with straight stitches.

Attach the cast-on edge of the ears to the head. Attach the head to the body. Using the fastened-off yarn end, sew the tail seam. Using the cast-on yarn end, work a gathering thread along the cast-on edge of the tail and draw up tightly without stuffing. Attach the tail to the body.

Otter

Materials:

5g (⅕oz) of fleecy DK (8-ply/light worsted) yarn in dark brown (A) and a small amount in white (B)

Small amount of 4-ply (fingering) yarn in black (C)

Two 4mm (⅛in) black beads

Black cotton thread

Toy stuffing

Needles:

3.5mm (UK 9 or 10, US 4) needles

Size:

10cm (4in) tall

Instructions:

Body

Using yarn A, cast on 9 sts.

Row 1 (WS): p to end.

Row 2: (kfb) to end (18 sts).

Row 3: p to end.

Row 4: join in yarn B, k4 (B), k10 (A), join in another strand of yarn B, k4 (B).

Rows 5–19: keeping colours correct and beg with a p row, work 15 rows in st st.

Row 20: cast off 4 sts using yarn A to cast off last st (B), k1 (A), k2tog (A), k2 (A), k2tog (A), k2 (A), cast off remaining 4 sts (B) (8 sts).

Continue using yarn A only.

Row 21: cast on 6 sts, p to end (14 sts).

Row 22: cast on 6 sts, k to end (20 sts).

Rows 23–25: beg with a p row, work 3 rows in st st.

Row 26: k6 (A), join in yarn B, k8 (B), join in another strand of yarn A, k6 (A).

Rows 27–28: keeping colours correct and beg with a p row, work 2 rows in st st.

Keeping colours correct, cast off.

Head

Using yarn A, cast on 8 sts.

Row 1 (WS): p to end.

Row 2: (kfb) to end (16 sts).

Rows 3–11: beg with a p row, work 9 rows in st st.

Row 12 (eyeline): k5, (k2tog) three times, k5 (13 sts).

Row 13: p to end.

Break off yarn A.

Rows 14–17: change to yarn B and beg with a k row, work 4 rows in st st.

Break yarn, draw through sts, pull tightly and fasten off.

Legs: make two

Using yarn A, cast on 10 sts.

Rows 1–3: beg with a p (WS) row, work 3 rows in st st.

Row 4: k3, (k2tog) twice, k3 (8 sts).

Rows 5–10: beg with a p row, work 6 rows in st st.

Break yarn, draw through sts, pull tightly and fasten off.

Ears: make two

Using yarn A, cast on 12 sts.

Break yarn, draw through sts, pull tightly and fasten off.

Sew the ends together to make a semi-circle.

Tail

Using yarn A, cast on 10 sts.

Rows 1–10: beg with a k (RS) row, work 10 rows in st st.

Break yarn, draw through sts, pull tightly and fasten off.

To make up

Using the cast-on yarn end, work a gathering thread along the cast-on edge of the body and draw up tightly. Using matching yarn, sew up the tummy seam. Fold each arm horizontally and sew each arm from the tip. Work a gathering thread along the tip of each arm and draw up tightly to close. Stuff the body and arms and sew the cast-off edge to the tummy edge.

Beginning at the fastened-off end, use matching yarn to sew up the head seam to half way. Using the cast-on yarn end, work a gathering thread along the cast-on edge and draw up tightly. Stuff the head and close the seam. Using yarn A, work a gathering thread over the eyeline and pull gently to shape. Attach the beads for the eyes. Attach the ears to the head. Using yarn C, embroider a nose and a mouth with straight stitches.

Attach the head to the body. Beginning at the fastened-off end, sew up each leg seam and stuff. Using the cast-on yarn end, work a gathering thread along the cast-on edge of each leg and draw up tightly to close. Attach this end of the legs to the body. Thread a length of yarn A up through the sole of one foot, bring it out at the top of the foot and repeat. Pull the thread gently to shape the ankle. Repeat for the other foot. Beginning at the fastened-off end, sew the tail seam and attach the cast-on edge of the tail to the body without stuffing.

Owl

Materials:

3g (1/10oz) of fleecy DK (8-ply/light worsted) yarn in dark brown or grey (A) and small amounts in light brown or white (B)

Small amounts of 4-ply (fingering) yarn in white (C) and dark brown (D)

Small amount of DK (8-ply/light worsted) yarn in khaki yellow (E)

Toy stuffing

Needles:

3.5mm (UK 9 or 10, US 4) and 3mm (UK 11, US 2 or 3) needles

Size:

8cm (3¼in) tall

Instructions:

Body

Using yarn A and 3.5mm (UK 9 or 10, US 4) needles, cast on 12 sts.

Row 1 (WS): p to end.

Row 2: (kfb) to end (24 sts).

Rows 3–17: beg with a p row, work 15 rows in st st.

Row 18: (k2, k2tog) to end (18 sts).

Rows 19–27: change to yarn B and beg with a p row, work 9 rows in st st.

Cast off.

Wings: make two

Using yarn A and 3.5mm (UK 9 or 10, US 4) needles, cast on 10 sts.

Rows 1 and 2: k 2 rows.

Row 3: skpo, k to last 2 sts, k2tog (8 sts).

Row 4: k to end.

Rows 5 and 6: repeat rows 3 and 4 (6 sts).

Row 7: (k2tog) to end (3 sts).

Break yarn, draw through sts, pull tightly and fasten off.

Eyes: make two

Using yarn C and 3mm (UK 11, US 2 or 3) needles, cast on 14 sts.

Row 1 (WS): p to end.

Row 2: (k2tog) to end (7 sts).

Break yarn, draw through sts, pull tightly and fasten off. Sew the sides together to make a circle.

Beak

Using yarn E and 3mm (UK 11, US 2 or 3) needles, cast on 5 sts.

Row 1 (WS): p2tog, p1, p2tog (3 sts).

Row 2: sl1, k2tog, pass the first st over the second st and fasten off.

To make up

Using the cast-on yarn end, work a gathering thread along the cast-on edge of the body and draw up tightly. Using matching yarn, sew up the body to the cast-off edge and stuff. With the seam at centre back, sew the cast-off edge together, pulling slightly to form the ears and closing the body.

Attach the eyes. Using yarn D, embroider the eyes with French knots and straight stitches, see the pictures for guidance. Attach the cast-on edge of the beak to the face. Using the fastened-off yarn end, sew the wing seams and attach the cast-on edge of each wing to the body without stuffing. Using yarn B, embroider dots on the body.

Hedgehog

Materials:

3g (¹⁄₁₀oz) of fleecy DK (8-ply/light worsted) yarn in cream (A)

3g (¹⁄₁₀oz) of eyelash chunky (bulky) yarn in light brown (B)

Small amount of DK (8-ply/light worsted) yarn in light brown (C)

Two 4mm (⅛in) black beads and black cotton thread

Toy stuffing

Needles:

3.5mm (UK 9 or 10, US 4) needles, 3mm (UK 11, US 2 or 3) needles and 4mm (UK 8, US 6) needles

Size:

7cm (2¾in) long

Instructions:

Body

Using yarn A and 3.5mm (UK 9 or 10, US 4) needles, cast on 9 sts.

Row 1 (WS): p to end.

Row 2: (kfb) to end (18 sts).

Row 3: p to end.

Row 4: (k1, kfb) to end (27 sts).

Rows 5–14: beg with a p row, work 10 rows in st st.

Row 15: (p1, p2tog) to end (18 sts).

Rows 16 and 17: beg with a k row, work 2 rows in st st.

Row 18: (k1, k2tog) to end (12 sts).

Rows 19 and 20: beg with a p row, work 2 rows in st st.

Row 21: (p1, p2tog) to end (8 sts).

Break yarn, draw through sts, pull tightly and fasten off.

Ears: make two

Using yarn C and 3mm (UK 11, US 2 or 3) needles, cast on 8 sts and purl 1 row.

Break yarn, draw through sts, pull tightly and fasten off.

Sew the ends together to make a semi-circle.

Arms: make two

Using yarn A and 3.5mm (UK 9 or 10, US 4) needles, cast on 6 sts.

Rows 1–4: beg with a p (WS) row, work 4 rows in st st.

Break yarn, draw through sts, pull tightly and fasten off.

Nose

Using yarn C and 3mm (UK 11, US 2 or 3) needles, cast on 6 sts.

Break yarn, draw through sts and pull tightly.

Sew the ends together to make a bobble.

Spikes

Using yarn B and 4mm (UK 8, US 6) needles, cast on 10 sts.

Row 1 (WS): p to end.

Row 2: (kfb) to end (20 sts).

Row 3: p to end.

Row 4: (k1, kfb) to end (30 sts).

Rows 5–11: beg with a p row, work 7 rows in st st.

Row 12: cast off 5 sts, k to end (25 sts).

Row 13: cast off 5 sts, p to end (20 sts).

Rows 14–17: beg with a k row, work 4 rows in st st.

Row 18: (k2, k2tog) to end (15 sts).

Rows 19–21: beg with a p row, work 3 rows in st st.

Row 22: (k1, k2tog) to end (10 sts).

Row 23: p to end.

Cast off.

To make up

Using the fastened-off yarn end, sew up the body seam to half way. Using the cast-on yarn end, work a gathering thread along the cast-on edge and draw up tightly. Sew up the body seam a little further, stuff and close the body.

Using yarn A, work a gathering thread where you want to create the neck and draw up tightly. Using the cast-on yarn end, sew up the seam for the spikes to row 13. Wrap the spikes around the body, covering the back of the body and placing the seam underneath the body. Stitch all around to secure the spikes.

Using the fastened-off yarn end, sew the arm seams. Attach the cast-on edge of the arms to the body without stuffing. Attach the beads for the eyes. Attach the nose. Using yarn C, embroider a mouth with a straight stitch. Attach the ears.

Squirrel

Materials:

Squirrel:

8g (⅓oz) of fleecy DK (8-ply/light worsted) yarn in orange and 3g (⅒oz) in white (B)

Small amount of DK (8-ply/light worsted) yarn in dark brown (C)

Two 4mm (⅛in) black beads and black cotton thread

Toy stuffing

Acorn:

Small amounts of DK (8-ply/light worsted) yarn in light brown (D) and dark brown (E)

Toy stuffing

Needles:

3.5mm (UK 9 or 10, US 4) needles and 3mm (UK 11, US 2 or 3) needles

Size:

Squirrel: 10cm (4in) tall; Acorn: 3cm (1⅛in) long

Instructions:

Body

Using yarn A and 3.5mm (UK 9 or 10, US 4) needles, cast on 10 sts.

Row 1 (WS): p to end.

Row 2: (kfb) to end (20 sts).

Row 3: join in yarn B, p4 (B), p12 (A), join in another strand of yarn B, p4 (B).

Rows 4–13: keeping colours correct and beg with a k row, work 10 rows in st st.

Row 14: cast off 4 sts using yarn A to cast off last st (B), k1 (A), (k2tog, k2) twice (A), k2tog (A), cast off remaining 4 sts (B) (9 sts).

Continue using yarn A only.

Row 15: cast on 5 sts, p to end (14 sts).

Row 16: cast on 5 sts, k to end (19 sts).

Rows 17–20: beg with a p row, work 4 rows in st st.

Row 21: cast off 4 sts, p to end (15 sts).

Cast off.

Legs: make two

Using yarn A and 3.5mm (UK 9 or 10, US 4) needles, cast on 6 sts.

Row 1 (WS): p to end.

Row 2: (kfb) to end (12 sts).

Rows 3–7: beg with a p row, work 5 rows in st st.

Row 8: (k2tog) to end (6 sts).

Rows 9–11: beg with a p row, work 3 rows in st st.

Break yarn, draw through sts, pull tightly and fasten off.

Head

Using yarn A and 3.5mm (UK 9 or 10, US 4) needles, cast on 8 sts.

Row 1 (WS): p to end.

Row 2: (kfb) to end (16 sts).

Rows 3–7: beg with a p row, work 5 rows in st st.

Row 8 (eyeline): k4, (k2tog) four times, k4 (12 sts).

Row 9: p to end.

Row 10: (k2, k2tog) to end (9 sts).

Break off yarn A.

Row 11: change to yarn B and p to end.

Row 12: (k1, k2tog) to end (6 sts).

Row 13: p to end.

Break yarn, draw through sts, pull tightly and fasten off.

Ears: make two

Using yarn A and 3.5mm (UK 9 or 10, US 4) needles, cast on 4 sts.

Rows 1 and 2: beg with a p (WS) row, work 2 rows in st st.

Row 3: (p2tog) twice, pass the first st over the second st and fasten off.

Tail

Using yarn A and 3.5mm (UK 9 or 10, US 4) needles, cast on 12 sts.

Rows 1–20: beg with a p (WS) row, work 20 rows in st st.

Row 21: (p2tog) to end (6 sts).

Break yarn, draw through sts, pull tightly and fasten off.

To make up

Using the cast-on yarn end, work a gathering thread along the cast-on edge of the body and draw up tightly. Using matching yarn, sew up the tummy seam.

Fold each arm horizontally and sew each arm from the tip. Work a gathering thread along the tip of each arm and draw up tightly to close. Stuff the body and arms and sew the cast-off edge to the tummy edge.

Beginning at the fastened-off end, use matching yarn to sew up the head seam to half way. Using the cast-on yarn end, work a gathering thread along the cast-on edge and draw up tightly. Stuff the head and close the seam.

Using yarn A, work a gathering thread over the eyeline and pull gently to shape. Attach the cast-on edge of the ears to the head. Pull the yarn at the tip of the ears to form points. Attach the beads for the eyes. Using yarn C, embroider a nose and a mouth with straight stitches.

Attach the head to the body. Beginning at the fastened-off end, sew up each leg seam and stuff. Attach the cast-on edge of the legs to the body. Beginning at the fastened-off end, sew the tail seam. With the seam underneath the tail, attach the cast-on edge to the body without stuffing.

Acorn

Using yarn D and 3mm (UK 11, US 2 or 3) needles, cast on 14 sts.

Rows 1–3: k 3 rows.

Break off yarn D.

Rows 4–8: change to yarn E and beg with a k (RS) row, work 5 rows in st st.

Row 9: (p2tog) to end (7 sts).

Row 10: (k2tog) to last st, k1 (4 sts).

Break yarn, draw through sts, pull tightly and fasten off.

To make up

Beginning at the fastened-off end, use matching yarn to sew the side seam. Stuff the acorn.

Using the cast-on yarn end, work a gathering thread along the cast-on edge and draw up tightly to close. Attach the acorn to the squirrel's hands.

Seal Pup

Materials:

5g (⅕oz) of fleecy DK (8-ply/light worsted) yarn in white (A)

Small amounts of DK (8-ply/light worsted) yarn in cream (B) and dark brown (C)

Small amount of 4-ply (fingering) yarn in grey (D)

Two 4mm (⅛in) black beads

Black cotton thread

Toy stuffing

Needles:

3.5mm (UK 9 or 10, US 4) needles and 3mm (UK 11, US 2 or 3) needles

Size:

12.5cm (5in) long

Instructions:

Body

Using yarn A and 3.5mm (UK 9 or 10, US 4) needles, cast on 10 sts.

Row 1 (WS): p to end.

Row 2: (kfb) to end (20 sts).

Row 3: p to end.

Row 4: (k1, kfb) to end (30 sts).

Rows 5–15: beg with a p row, work 11 rows in st st.

Row 16: k2, (k2tog, k2) to end (23 sts).

Rows 17–23: beg with a p row, work 7 rows in st st.

Row 24: k2tog, (k1, k2tog) to end (15 sts).

Rows 25–31: beg with a p row, work 7 rows in st st.

Row 32: (k1, k2tog) to end (10 sts).

Break yarn, draw through sts, pull tightly and fasten off.

Tail

Using yarn A and 3.5mm (UK 9 or 10, US 4) needles, cast on 16 sts.

Rows 1 and 2: beg with a p (WS) row, work 2 rows in st st.

Row 3: p8, turn.

Work on this set of 8 sts only.

Row 4: skpo, k to last 2 sts, k2tog (6 sts).

Row 5: p2tog, p2, p2tog (4 sts).

Row 6: skpo, k2tog (2 sts).

Row 7: p2tog and fasten off.

With WS facing, rejoin yarn A to the other set of 8 sts and repeat rows 3–7.

Flippers: make two

Using yarn A and 3.5mm (UK 9 or 10, US 4) needles, cast on 10 sts.

Rows 1–5: beg with a p (WS) row, work 5 rows in st st.

Row 6: k2, (k2tog, k2) to end (8 sts).

Break yarn, draw through sts, pull tightly and fasten off.

Muzzle

Using yarn B and 3mm (UK 11, US 2 or 3) needles, cast on 16 sts.

Rows 1 and 2: beg with a p (WS) row, work 2 rows in st st.

Row 3: (p2tog) to end (8 sts).

Break yarn, draw through sts, pull tightly and fasten off.

To make up

Using the fastened-off yarn end, sew up the body seam to half way. Using the cast-on yarn end, work a gathering thread along the cast-on edge and draw up tightly. Sew up the body seam a little further, stuff and close the body.

Using the fastened-off yarn end, sew the muzzle seam. Insert a little toy stuffing and attach the cast-on edge of the muzzle to the face. Using the fastened-off yarn end, sew up each flipper seam. Attach the cast-on edge of the flippers to the body without stuffing. Fold in the sides of the tail to meet at the centre back and sew the seams. Attach the cast-on edge of the tail to the body without stuffing.

Attach the beads for the eyes. Using yarn C, embroider a nose and a mouth with straight stitches. Using yarn D, embroider small French knots on the muzzle.

Robin

Materials:

5g (⅕oz) of fleecy DK (8-ply/light worsted) yarn in dark brown (A) and small amounts in red (B) and light brown (C)

Small amounts of DK (8-ply/light worsted) yarn in dark brown (D), white (E), red (F) and pale blue (G)

Two 4mm (⅛in) black beads and black cotton thread

Toy stuffing

Needles:

3.5mm (UK 9 or 10, US 4) needles and 3mm (UK 11, US 2 or 3) needles

Size:

7cm (2¾in) tall, including hat

Instructions:

Body

Using yarn A and 3.5mm (UK 9 or 10, US 4) needles, cast on 10 sts.
Row 1 (WS): p to end.
Row 2: (kfb) to end (20 sts).
Row 3: p to end.
Row 4: k2, (kfb, k2) to end (26 sts).
Row 5: p7 (A), join in yarn C, p12 (C), p7 (A).
Rows 6–9: keeping the colours correct and beg with a k row, work 4 rows in st st.
Row 10: k7 (A), k4 (C), join in yarn B, k4 (B), k4 (C), k7 (A).
Row 11: p7 (A), p3 (C), p6 (B), p3 (C), p7 (A).
Row 12: k7 (A), k2 (C), k8 (B), k2 (C), k7 (A).
Row 13: p7 (A), p1 (C), p10 (B), p1 (C), p7 (A).
Break off yarn C.
Row 14: k7 (A), k12 (B), k7 (A).
Row 15: keeping the colours correct, p to end.
Row 16: keeping the colours correct, k2tog, k to last 2 sts, k2tog (24 sts).
Row 17: keeping the colours correct, p2tog, p to last 2 sts, p2tog (22 sts).
Row 18: keeping the colours correct, k2tog, k to last 2 sts, k2tog (20 sts).
Break off yarn B and continue using yarn A only.
Rows 19–23: beg with a p row, work 5 rows in st st.
Row 24: (k2, k2tog) to end (15 sts).

Row 25: p to end.
Row 26: (k1, k2tog) to end (10 sts).
Break yarn, draw through sts, pull tightly and fasten off.

Wings: make two

Using yarn A and 3.5mm (UK 9 or 10, US 4) needles, cast on 6 sts.
Rows 1–7: k 7 rows.
Row 8: k1, (k2tog) twice, k1 (4 sts).
Row 9: k to end.
Row 10: skpo, k2tog (2 sts).
Row 11: k2tog and fasten off.

Beak

Using yarn D and 3mm (UK 11, US 2 or 3) needles, cast on 5 sts.
Row 1 (WS): p to end.
Row 2: k2tog, k1, k2tog (3 sts).
Row 3: p1, p2tog (2 sts).
Row 4: k2tog and fasten off.

Hat

Using yarn G and 3mm (UK 11, US 2 or 3) needles, cast on 26 sts.
Rows 1 and 2: (k1, p1) to end.
Rows 3 and 4: change to yarn E and beg with a k (RS) row, work 2 rows in st st.
Rows 5 and 6: change to yarn F and beg with a k row, work 2 rows in st st.
Row 7: change to yarn G, k2tog, (k1, k2tog) to end (17 sts).
Row 8: using yarn G, p to end.
Row 9: change to yarn E, k2tog, (k1, k2tog) to end (11 sts).

Row 10: using yarn E, p1, (p2tog) to end (6 sts).
Break yarn, draw through sts, pull tightly and fasten off.
Note: Colour variation for the other hat:
Rows 1 and 2: using yarn E.
Rows 3 and 4: using yarn F.
Rows 5 and 6: using yarn G.
Rows 7 and 8: using yarn E.
Rows 9 and 10: using yarn F.

Bobble

Using yarn G and 3mm (UK 11, US 2 or 3) needles, cast on 8 sts.
Rows 1–5: beg with a p (WS) row, work 5 rows in st st.
Break yarn, draw through sts, pull tightly and fasten off.
Note: Colour variation for the other bobble: use yarn F.

To make up

Using the fastened-off yarn end, sew up the body seam to half way. Using the cast-on yarn end, work a gathering thread along the cast-on edge and draw up tightly. Sew up the body seam a little further, stuff and close the body.

Thread a length of yarn A up through the base of the body, bring it out at the spine and repeat. Pull the thread gently to shape.

Attach the cast-on edge of each wing to the body. Using the fastened-off yarn end, sew the beak seam. Attach the cast-on edge of the beak to the face. Attach the beads for the eyes.

Using the fastened-off yarn end, sew up the sides of the bobble and stuff. Work a gathering thread along the cast-on edge and draw up tightly to close the bobble. Sew up the hat seam. Attach the bobble to the hat, leaving the bobble hanging on a 1cm (½in) length of matching yarn. Attach the hat to the robin's head.

Raccoon

Materials:

7g (¼oz) of fleecy DK (8-ply/light worsted) yarn in grey (A) and small amounts in white (B) and soft brown (C)

Small amount of 4-ply (fingering) yarn in dark brown (D)

Two 6mm (¼in) black beads

Black cotton thread

Toy stuffing

Needles:

3.5mm (UK 9 or 10, US 4) needles

Size:

15cm (6in) long, including tail

Instructions:

Body

Using yarn A, cast on 10 sts.

Row 1 (WS): p to end.

Row 2: (kfb) to end (20 sts).

Row 3: p to end.

Row 4: k2, (kfb, k2) to end (26 sts).

Rows 5–13: beg with a p row, work 9 rows in st st.

Row 14: k2, (k2tog, k2) to end (20 sts).

Rows 15–17: beg with a p row, work 3 rows in st st.

Row 18: cast off 3 sts, k to end (17 sts).

Row 19: cast off 3 sts, p to end (14 sts).

Row 20: cast on 5 sts, k to end (19 sts).

Row 21: cast on 5 sts, p to end (24 sts).

Rows 22–27: beg with a k row, work 6 rows in st st.

Cast off.

Head

Work as for the body to row 4 (26 sts).

Rows 5–7: beg with a p row, work 3 rows in st st.

Row 8: k6 (A), join in yarn B, k14 (B), k6 (A).

Row 9: keeping colours correct, p to end.

Break off yarn B.

Row 10 (eyeline): k6 (A), join in yarn C, (k2tog, k4) twice (C), k2tog (C), k6 (A) (23 sts).

Rows 11 and 12: keeping colours correct and beg with a p row, work 2 rows in st st.

Break off yarn C and continue using yarn A only.

Row 13: p to end.

Break off yarn A.

Row 14: change to yarn B, (k2tog, k1) to last 2 sts, k2tog (15 sts).

Row 15: (p1, p2tog) to end (10 sts).

Rows 16 and 17: beg with a k row, work 2 rows in st st.

Break yarn, draw through sts, pull tightly and fasten off.

Ears: make two

Using yarn A, cast on 5 sts.

Row 1 (WS): p to end.

Row 2: skpo, k1, k2tog (3 sts).

Row 3: p1, p2tog (2 sts).

Row 4: k2tog and fasten off.

Tail

Using yarn C, cast on 12 sts.

Rows 1–3: beg with a p (WS) row, work 3 rows in st st.

Rows 4–7: change to yarn B and beg with a k row, work 4 rows in st st.

Row 8: change to yarn C, (k2, k2tog) to end (9 sts).

Rows 9–11: using yarn C and beg with a p row, work 3 rows in st st.

Rows 12–15: change to yarn B and beg with a k row, work 4 rows in st st.

Rows 16–18: change to yarn C and beg with a k row, work 3 rows in st st.

Break yarn, draw through sts, pull tightly and fasten off.

To make up

Using the cast-on yarn end, work a gathering thread along the cast-on edge of the body and draw up tightly. Sew up the tummy seam. Fold each front leg horizontally and sew each front leg from the tip. Work a gathering thread along the tip of each front leg and draw up tightly to close.

Stuff the body and front legs and sew the cast-off edge to the tummy edge. Secure each front leg to the body with a few stitches.

Beginning at the fastened-off end, use matching yarn to sew up the head seam to half way. Using the cast-on end yarn, work a gathering thread along the cast-on edge and draw up tightly. Stuff the head and close the seam. Using yarn C, work a gathering thread over the eyeline and pull gently to shape. Attach the cast-on edge of the ears to the head. Attach the beads for the eyes. Using yarn D, embroider a nose with straight stitches. Attach the head to the body.

Beginning at the fastened-off end of the tail, use matching yarn to sew up the tail seam. Stuff the tail and attach the cast-on edge to the body.

Fat Cat

Materials:

3g (1/10oz) of fleecy DK (8-ply/light worsted) yarn in grey (A) and a small amount in white (B)

Small amounts of 4-ply (fingering) yarn in light brown (C) and dark brown (D)

Toy stuffing

Needles:

3.5mm (UK 9 or 10, US 4) needles

Size:

8cm (3¼in) tall

Instructions:

Body

Using yarn A, cast on 10 sts.

Row 1 (WS): p to end.

Row 2: (kfb) to end (20 sts).

Row 3: p to end.

Row 4: k2, (kfb, k2) to end (26 sts).

Row 5: p7 (A), join in yarn B, p12 (B), p7 (A).

Rows 6 and 7: keeping colours correct and beg with a k row, work 2 rows in st st.

Row 8: k8 (A), k10 (B), k8 (A).

Rows 9–11: keeping colours correct and beg with a p row, work 3 rows in st st.

Row 12: k9 (A), k8 (B), k9 (A).

Rows 13–15: keeping colours correct and beg with a p row, work 3 rows in st st.

Row 16: keeping colours correct, k2, (k2tog, k2) to end (20 sts).

Row 17: p7 (A), p6 (B), p7 (A).

Rows 18 and 19: keeping colours correct and beg with a k row, work 2 rows in st st.

Break off yarn B and continue using yarn A only.

Rows 20–25: beg with a k row, work 6 rows in st st.

Row 26: (k2tog) to end (10 sts).

Break yarn, draw through sts, pull tightly and fasten off.

Ears: make two

Using yarn A, cast on 5 sts.

Row 1 (WS): p to end.

Row 2: skpo, k1, k2tog (3 sts).

Row 3: sl1, p2tog (2 sts).

Row 4: k2tog and fasten off.

Muzzle

Using yarn B, cast on 14 sts.

Row 1 (WS): p to end.

Row 2: (k2tog) to end (7 sts).

Break yarn, draw through sts, pull tightly and fasten off.

Tail

Using yarn A, cast on 15 sts.

Rows 1–4: beg with a p (WS) row, work 4 rows in st st.

Cast off.

To make up

Using the fastened-off yarn end, sew up the body seam to half way. Using the cast-on yarn end, work a gathering thread along the cast-on edge and draw up tightly. Sew up the body seam a little further, stuff and close the body.

Attach the cast-on edge of the ears to the head. Using the fastened-off yarn end, sew the muzzle seam. Insert a little toy stuffing and attach the cast-on edge of the muzzle to the face.

Sew up the tail seam. Work a gathering thread along each end of the tail and draw up tightly to close. Attach the tail to the body.

Using yarn D, embroider the eyes, a nose and a mouth with straight stitches. Using yarn C, embroider the whiskers with straight stitches.

Puppy

Materials:

To make one:

5g (⅕oz) of fleecy DK (8-ply/light worsted) yarn in grey, dark brown or light brown (A) and a small amount in white (B)

Small amounts of DK (8-ply/light worsted) yarn in dark brown (C) and black (D)

Toy stuffing

Needles:

3.5mm (UK 9 or 10, US 4) needles

Size:

11cm (4¼in) long including tail

Instructions:

Body

For all puppies: using yarn A, cast on 20 sts.

Rows 1–10: beg with a k (RS) row, work 10 rows in st st.

Row 11: cast off 4 sts, k to end (16 sts).

Row 12: cast off 4 sts, p to end (12 sts).

Row 13: cast on 2 sts, k to end (14 sts).

Row 14: cast on 2 sts, p to end (16 sts).

Rows 15–18: beg with a k row, work 4 rows in st st.

Row 19: cast off 2 sts, k to end (14 sts).

Row 20: cast off 2 sts, p to end (12 sts).

Row 21: cast on 8 sts, knit these 8 sts, (k2tog, k2) to end (17 sts).

Row 22: cast on 8 sts, p to end (25 sts).

Rows 23–28: beg with a k row, work 6 rows in st st.

Cast off.

Ears: make two

Using yarn A, cast on 6 sts.

Rows 1 and 2: beg with a k (RS) row, work 2 rows in st st.

Row 3: (k2tog, k1) to end (4 sts).

Row 4: p to end.

Cast off.

Tail

Using yarn A, cast on 6 sts.

Rows 1–4: beg with a p (WS) row, work 4 rows in st st.

Row 5: (p2tog) to end (3 sts).

Row 6: k3tog and fasten off.

Head

For the golden retriever and miniature French poodle: using yarn A, cast on 10 sts.

Row 1 (WS): p to end.

Row 2: (kfb) to end (20 sts).

Rows 3–7: beg with a p row, work 5 rows in st st.

Row 8 (eyeline): k4, (k2tog) six times, k4 (14 sts).

Rows 9–12: beg with a p row, work 4 rows in st st.

Row 13: (p2tog) to end (7 sts).

Break yarn, draw through sts, pull tightly and fasten off.

Head

For the Schnauzer: work as for the golden retriever and the miniature French poodle to row 8 (14 sts).

Row 9: p to end.

Break off yarn A.

Rows 10–13: change to yarn B and beg with a k row, work 4 rows in st st.

Row 14: k2tog, (k1, k2tog) to end (9 sts).

Break yarn, draw through sts, pull tightly and fasten off.

To make up

Fold each leg horizontally and sew each leg from the tip. Work a gathering thread along the tip of each leg and draw up tightly to close. Stuff the legs.

Sew up the tummy seam leaving a gap for stuffing. Stuff and close the body. Using the fastened-off yarn end and matching yarn, sew up the head seam to half way. Using the cast-on yarn end, work a gathering thread along the cast-on edge and draw up tightly. Stuff the head and close the seam. Using yarn A, work a gathering thread over the eyeline and pull gently to shape. Attach the cast-on edge of the ears to the head.

For the golden retriever and the Schnauzer, use yarn C to embroider French knots for the eyes and to embroider a nose with straight stitches. For the French poodle, use yarn D to embroider French knots for the eyes and to embroider a nose with straight stitches. For the Schnauzer, use yarn B to embroider the eyebrows with a straight stitch. Attach the head to the body.

Sew the legs into position with a few stitches, see the pictures for guidance. Sew the tail seam and attach the tail to the body without stuffing.

Duck & Ducklings

Materials:

7g (¼oz) of fleecy DK (8-ply/light worsted) yarn in white (A) and a small amount in yellow (B)

Small amounts of 4-ply (fingering) yarn in mustard (C) and dark brown (D)

Small amount of DK (8-ply/light worsted) yarn in dark mustard (E)

Patterned cotton fabric, 16cm (6¼in) x 6cm (2½in)

Two 4mm (⅛in) black beads

Black cotton thread

Toy stuffing

Needles:

3.5mm (UK 9 or 10, US 4) needles and 3mm (UK 11, US 2 or 3) needles

Size:

Duck: 9cm (3½in) tall; duckling: 3cm (1¼in) tall

Instructions:

Duck

Body

Using yarn A and 3.5mm (UK 9 or 10, US 4) needles, cast on 10 sts.

Row 1 (WS): p to end.
Row 2: (kfb) to end (20 sts).
Row 3: p to end.
Row 4: k2, (kfb, k2) to end (26 sts).
Row 5: p to end.
Row 6: k2tog, k10, (kfb) twice, k10, k2tog (26 sts).
Row 7: p to end.
Rows 8–15: rep rows 6 and 7 four times.
Rows 16–27: beg with a k row, work 12 rows in st st.
Row 28: k5, (k2tog, k1) five times, k2tog, k4 (20 sts).
Rows 29–31: beg with a p row, work 3 rows in st st.
Row 32: k5, (k2tog) five times, k5 (15 sts).
Rows 33–41: beg with a p row, work 9 rows in st st.

Break yarn, draw through sts, pull tightly and fasten off.

Wings: make two

Using yarn A and 3.5mm (UK 9 or 10, US 4) needles, cast on 9 sts.

Rows 1–7: beg with a p (WS) row, work 7 rows in st st.
Row 8: k2, k2tog, k1, k2tog, k2 (7 sts).
Row 9: p to end.
Row 10: k2, k2tog, k3 (6 sts).

Row 11: p to end.
Row 12: k2, k2tog, k2 (5 sts).
Row 13: p to end.
Cast off.

Beak

Using yarn C and 3mm (UK 11, US 2 or 3) needles, cast on 12 sts.

Row 1 (WS): p to end.
Row 2: (k2, k2tog) to end (9 sts).
Row 3: (p2tog) to last st, p1 (5 sts).

Break yarn, draw through sts, pull tightly and fasten off.

Feet: make two

Using yarn E and 3mm (UK 11, US 2 or 3) needles, cast on 5 sts.

Rows 1–5: k 5 rows.
Row 6: skpo, k1, k2tog (3 sts).
Row 7: k to end.
Cast off.

Headscarf

Cut the patterned cotton fabric into a triangle, 16 x 10 x 10cm (6¼ x 4 x 4in). Fold under 1cm (½in) of fabric on all three sides and stitch down to create a hem all around and ties.

To make up

Using the fastened-off yarn end, sew up the body seam to half way. Using the cast-on yarn end, work a gathering thread along the cast-on edge and draw up tightly. Sew up the body seam a little further, stuff and close the body.

Attach the cast-on edge of the wings to the body. Attach the cast-off edge of the feet to the body. Using the fastened-off yarn end, sew the beak seam and attach the cast-on edge of the beak to the face. Using yarn D, embroider the nostrils on top of the beak with straight stitches. Attach the beads for the eyes. Wrap the headscarf around the head and tie it in a knot under the chin.

Duckling

Body

Using yarn B and 3.5mm (UK 9 or 10, US 4) needles, cast on 6 sts.

Row 1 (WS): p to end.
Row 2: (kfb) to end (12 sts).
Rows 3–7: beg with a p row, work 5 rows in st st.
Row 8: cast off 3 sts, k to end (9 sts).
Row 9: cast off 3 sts, p to end (6 sts).
Row 10: kfb, k to last st, kfb (8 sts).
Rows 11 and 12: beg with a p row, work 2 rows in st st.

Break yarn, draw through sts, pull tightly and fasten off.

Beak

Using yarn C and 3mm (UK 11, US 2 or 3) needles, cast on 3 sts.

Row 1: p1, p2tog, pass the first st over the second st and fasten off.

To make up

Using the fastened-off yarn end, sew up the body seam to half way. Using the cast-on yarn end, work a gathering thread along the cast-on edge and draw up tightly. Sew up the body seam a little further, stuff and close the body. Attach the cast-on edge of the beak to the face. Using yarn D, embroider French knots for the eyes.

Acknowledgements

I would like to thank everyone on the Search Press team, especially Katie French and May Corfield, for helping me to create such a wonderful book. I would also like to thank the designers, Juan Hayward and Emma Sutcliffe, for the beautiful layout and the photographer, Fiona Murray, for the lovely photography. Thanks also go to Jacky Edwards for her pattern checking.